Adopt Adapt

Achieve

---

*An Amazing Triple A Guide for Successful
Relocation, Change and Integration*

∞

EPHRAIM OSAGHAE MBL, PMP, MBA

Author of *A Handbook for Migrants* and *Voices from Home*

ISBN (Paperback):   978-0-6484799-5-6
ISBN (eBook):   978-0-6484799-6-3

DEDICATION

To immigrants, locals and the multicultural world...
and all that makes the change more worthwhile

Acknowledgement

I want to thank Monica Martin, Malcolm and Jill Innes, Cornelius Itotoh, and Lakshmi Kanchi for kindly using part of their precious time and efforts to read the manuscripts, or parts thereof, of this book. Their critique and feedback have contributed to enriching the final version.

My special acknowledgement goes to friends, colleagues and members in various organisations in the community, business and governmental sectors. The valuable interactions with them and other stakeholders have contributed to the information, experiences and inspiration for writing this book.

Finally, I would like to appreciate my family for the ongoing partnership and support in this educating, challenging and rewarding adventure of relocation, change and integration.

Table of Contents

1. The Need For A Guide

Everyone regularly needs guidance in life. It could be in the form of being shown the way, especially by others that have navigated the same path thereby avoiding pitfalls and pains while maximizing gains along the way. Guidance could also be provided as valuable information or advice which will help in the formation of opinions or in making decisions. Finally, it could be presented as signposts to direct motion and positioning to help maintain and keep within the set pathway. What if all these are packaged and delivered in a book that can be simple, reusable and transferable?

Immigration is an important endeavour that warrants guidance in many respects to achieve a successful outcome. The Immigration Department of the host country will typically own the entire immigration process, including the specific categories, countries of origin, frequency of visa programs, and the number of intakes. They will also determine the eligibility and the ultimate approval for those who they are accepting as immigrants. Even they are guided.

There are other parties involved in the immigration value chain. They include nominating employers (where applicable), immigration agents, service providers that support immigrants on arrival for their settlement, etc.

All these stakeholders are guided, using government and private sector legislation, regulations, guidelines and protocols in their work within this space of immigration. Whilst they will definitely enjoy some benefits from reading this book, the focus and target audience are immigrants themselves – the intending, new, and established immigrants. They need guidance. They need to hear and read the stories of others that have gone ahead of them – the good, the challenges and the lessons. They will also be gainfully guided by information, direction, and leadership – the type of information and anecdotal experiences that will not necessarily duplicate those received from relevant government agencies, immigration agents and service providers.

Rather they need intelligence that will come from lived experiences of immigrants that have walked the path that they are currently anticipating to get on sooner or later. This is what this book delivers. It provides the immigrant with guidance especially in the following key aspects:

- How to prepare for the relocation including the need to articulate and cherish their 'Whys' for the big move, and anticipated changes ahead.

- How to adopt the new country and residence because of the need to achieve and sustain the right balance between the prevailing sociocultural norms and the immigrants' own cultural background and uniqueness.

- How to adapt and remain relevant in the new domain while maintaining their competitive edge in dealing with change.

- How to achieve their set goals while integrating and contributing to national growth in their new country.

- How to undertake the steps above in the context of three key and interrelated aspects of life – family, career and ageing.

The importance of the work of specialists in the areas of family therapy, career counselling, and ageing is fully recognised. However, these services cannot replace the benefits of guidance based on lived experiences. The combined use of theory and experience will ultimately be more robustly practical and effective.

Remarkably though, the growing evidence of ongoing challenges in these aspects of life for most immigrants, have warranted further guidance and actions. There is an increasing need to shift more of the immigrant's frustrating experiences to more rewarding and sustainable successes. The incentives for efforts towards this goal should not rest with just the immigrants themselves but all stakeholders should support, encourage and facilitate such works. After all, more successful immigrants will invariably result in more benefits across the value chain including growth in national wealth of the countries where these immigrants now call home. This is the main reason for this book. It is to be used as a guide.

The Target Audience

Intending immigrants need to read the book, reflect on key aspects, and use it as a guide for setting goals and action plans as part of their preparations for emigration. They have the best opportunities to save themselves many of the mistakes and pain that others like the author of this book have already experienced. Some of these experiences are included in this book.

New and settled immigrants, including *international students*, also need to take the same approach in using this guide as intending migrants except that their case is not about preparations to migrate. Rather, it is about taking the next decisive steps to ensure success in their aspirations regarding family, career and ageing. There is still time for them to make necessary changes that will set them on their path for achieving their goals.

Policy and lawmakers will find useful hints and tips from reading this book that will further help them when developing and formulating policies and passing laws that will ensure considerations for real diversity and inclusion in matters relating to family, career and ageing. While people that have immigrated into the country embark on efforts to adopt and adapt in the context of the new country, they can be further supported by the adjustment to current, and the creation of, new policies and laws that will more meaningfully complement their efforts without compromising the welfare of other members of the community. Policy and lawmakers are aware of the economic benefits that immigrants bring to their countries. Being aware of the immigrant's particular challenges could help inform them to further support their efforts to settle quicker, better and more sustainably, for the good of all stakeholders. This book can contribute to providing that awareness.

Local residents, students and professionals can read, reflect and develop the necessary cultural intelligence which has become of increasingly high demand considering the cultural diversity in our neighbourhoods, schools and workplaces.

Other key stakeholders in the immigration context will find that this book will contribute to their overall knowledge on the subject matter, as well as providing them with key reference materials for their daily endeavours.

Some of the principles in this book also apply to many other change contexts involving some form of relocation and integration. International students, expats, diplomatic attaché, etc. will still have to consider aspects of their families, careers, and ageing depending on their individual circumstances.

Some information of historical value and facts are presented next to provide some context.

2. Some Background Information

Immigrants – intending, new, emerging and settled – will particularly find the content of this book very useful. However, the life principles and lessons will be applicable for everyone interested in families, careers and ageing. After all, we all place much value on these aspects of our lives, though with varying degrees of attention.

The case studies will have contexts of Australia as the new country of the immigrant country and Africa as the homeland and cultural background of the immigrant. The choice of using African-Australians for the case study is mainly to ensure that the stories are real and not

> *'I may not have gone where I intended to go, but I think I have ended up where I intended to be'- Douglas Adams*

fictional as most of the author's life and experiences are situated in this context. Again, it has to be emphasized that the stories are relatable to other immigration contexts and the principles and lessons will apply across the board most of the times.

Noteworthy exceptions and cautions against over-generalisation will be highlighted where applicable.

Let us revisit the question which has divided many in the past: Who is an immigrant? Simply, he or she is a person who relocates from his or her country of birth to another country to settle down and reside over a long period or permanently.

Australia has grown to become an enviable example of a multicultural country. Though some parts of the history of how the country got to where it is today do trigger different types of emotions depending on your place and ancestry in the history. Therefore, we will focus on the aspects of historical facts that are relevant to the subject matter of this book – how to be more successful at adoption and adaptation that will ensure achievement of immigrant's goals most of the time.

It is a fact that Australia is a multicultural country with a significant number of immigrants from various countries: 7.5 million (29.7%) of the 25.366

million people living in Australian as at 2019 are born overseas. [1]

However, we can learn so much from the history and timeline of how the country got to where it is today in terms of immigration. The snapshot from the work jointly developed by World Vision Australia and the Primary English Teaching Association Australia provides some highlights. Arguably, the timeline shows that all Australians are immigrants or their ancestors were immigrants. The indigenous people, namely Aboriginal and Torres Strait Islanders are the only exceptions.

[1] 3412.0 - Migration, Australia, 2018-19, Released by Australian Bureau of Statistics (ABS) 28/04/2020, www.abs.gov.au

1700	1788	1851	1860	1870
Indigenous population estimated at 300,000–750,000.	From 1788-1868, 160,000 convicts were shipped to the Australian colonies from the United Kingdom. From the early 1790s, free immigrants also began coming to Australia.	During the Gold Rush era of 1851 to 1860, around 500,000 people migrated to Australia. The main migrant communities were from England, Ireland, Scotland, Wales, China and the USA.	From 1860–1900, labourers from Melanesia (Pacific Islands) were recruited to work on Queensland sugar plantations.	From 1850–1900, Afghani, Pakistani and Turkish camel handlers played an important part in opening up central Australia, helping in the building of telegraph and railway lines.

1880	1901	1950	1956	1968
In the late 1800s, Japanese fishers were important in the pearling industry.	1901 – With Federation, the Immigration Restriction Act was passed which made it very difficult for non-English speaking immigrants to come to Australia. This was the beginning of the White Australia Policy that existed until 1973.	After World War II, during the 1950 and 1960s, large numbers of migrants came to Australia from the Netherlands, Greece, Italy, Malta, Germany and Turkey. This was part of the 'Populate or Perish' migration policy.	In 1956, Hungarian refugees fled fighting in their country.	In 1968, Czech refugees fled fighting.

1973	1975	1976	2000	
In 1973, refugees came to Australia from Chile following the overthrow of the elected government.	From 1975-1985, over 90,000 refugees came to Australia from Indochina (Vietnam, Cambodia and Laos) after the end of the Vietnam War.	From 1976–1981, approximately 16,000 Lebanese refugees fled civil war.	From 2000, Australia has taken in people from a broad range of countries including Iraq, Myanmar, Afghanistan, Sudan, India and Sri Lanka. However, the majority of settlers are from New Zealand and the UK.	

Timeline of Immigration in Australia[2]

While people from Europe account for a significant proportion of the total number of immigrants in Australia, the rate of intake from Asia has been highest over the past few years mostly driven by

---

[2] World Vision Australia 2012 (http://www.globalwords.edu.au/, accessed 9/6/2020)

arrivals from India and China. There are relatively modest intakes from Africa and the Americas.

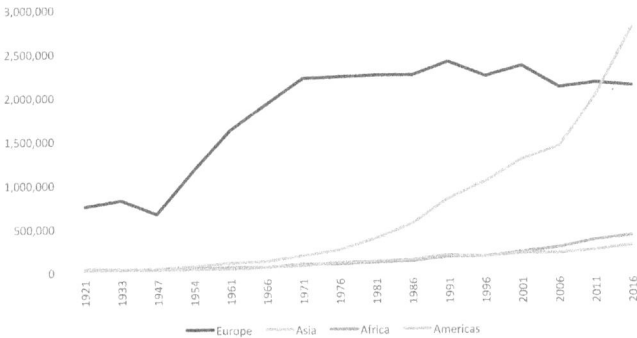

Migrants to Australia by region of origin, 1921 to 2016[3]

The other fact worth stating here is that most permanent migration visas have been given to skilled migrants relative to family and humanitarian categories. Indeed, countries like Australia that open their doors to accept immigrants do have their own goals. In this case, they prefer young and highly skilled immigrants with a higher probability of contributing to national economic development. The leaders and policymakers have to ask themselves as well: '*What is in it for us as a nation?*'

---

[3] Bankwest Curtin Economic Centre, Finding A Place To Call Home. Focus on the States Series, No. 7/19, November 2019 P.6

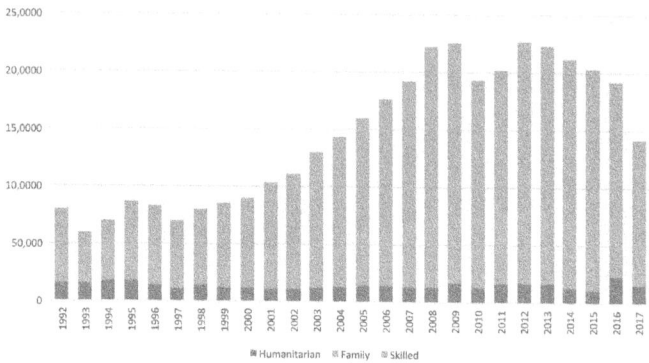

Source: Bankwest Curtin Economics Centre | Authors' calculations based on Department of Home Affairs, Settlement Database (SDB)

New permanent migration to Australia by visa stream, 1992-2016[4]

Going forward, these immigrants now call their new country their home. As illustrated with the case of Australia above, they mostly take the giant leap, many times into the unknown for many reasons. Again, using the Australian context, work and career, family connections and reunion, and humanitarian (asylum, protection, etc.) are the main reasons according to the reported visa streams. But how much progress has been made in these aspects of immigrants' lives? Let us consider some key facts about family, career and ageing.

---

[4] Bankwest Curtin Economic Centre, Finding A Place To Call Home. Focus on the States Series, No. 7/19, November 2019 P.7

Family life is one area with mixed results when it comes to the subject of outcomes for immigrants. The outcomes have been great in some areas like enjoying a stable economic and secured environment for the family. But other areas need urgent and decisive interventions, with the immigrant families themselves leading the change. The situation is further complicated because family life is a complex aspect to investigate. However the well-meaning intentions are, there is a need to respect implied and real private spaces associated with this important unit of any community and country. Many times, community and government leaders are only able to deal with lagging outcomes, like domestic violence, incarceration, and divorce and the ripple effects they cause in the community and future generations ahead. Prevention is better than cure so there could be more sustainable solutions with proactively investing time, efforts and other resources in dealing with leading issues. Again, we will use facts in Australia as the case study to illustrate further.

Family and domestic violence (FDV) 'is the intentional and systematic use of violence and abuse to control, coerce or create fear.' [5]

The issue of FDV has increasingly become a major cause for concern in Australia. However, there is limited data for highlighting the specific aspects relating to immigrants. Thankfully, there is data regarding aspects of incarceration and divorce.

Whilst about 30% (almost 1 in 3) of all Australians are immigrants, they accounted for about 17% (almost 1 in 5) of those in prison between 30 June 2018 and 30 June 2019[6]. The situation looks okay in relative terms. However, no one would wish for anyone to be incarcerated, especially family members. It will be interesting to compare similar statistics in other countries like Canada that share some similarities with Australia in terms of multiculturalism.

---

[5] ref: https://www.dcp.wa.gov.au/CrisisAndEmergency/FDV/Pages/Whatisfamilyanddomesticviolence.aspx
[6] 5B 4517.0 - Prisoners in Australia, 2019, Released by ABS 05/12/2019

What is the situation like with marriages and divorces? In 2018, there were 49,404 registered divorces in Australia. Approximately 51% and 49% involved non-immigrants and immigrants respectively based on data from ABS. It is even more remarkable that while the rate of divorce amongst locally born Australian married couples dropped during the 2017 to 2018 period, those of immigrants increased during the same period. It is noted however that there could be more complex explanations for this trend which are beyond the scope of this book.

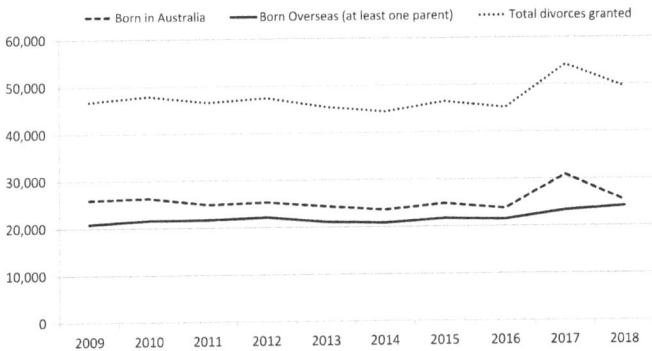

People granted divorce in the last 10 years in Australia (ABS 2020)[7]

---

[7] ABS 3310.0 - Marriages and Divorces, Australia, 2018 (Released 27/11/2019 www.abs.gov.au).

Now let us make one important statement here: the intent of this section is not to defame anyone that has been through divorce or people that have been affected by such a situation. No one can really boast that much when it comes to the institution of marriage. However, it is a rational expectation that people go into marriage with the expectation that it will last a lifetime. Thus, the current trend deserves some attention in trying to force the curve to go down. The situation does call for more guidance for immigrants, especially those that would want to give their marriage the best shot of not contributing to the statistics of marital breakdowns and all the associated pains. Let us proceed to consider some other facts. This time, it is about immigrants and career.

Most statistics have shown increase participation in work for immigrants over time. This is worth acknowledging although there have been many shocks along the way like the global financial crisis in 2009, the oil price slump 2014 – 2016 and COVID-19 pandemic 2020. Unfortunately, many immigrants do bear the direct impact of these situations, mostly due to other particular challenges, which will be presented in details in the main section on Career in this book. But the facts that will be the focus here, concern the following question: 'Are the hard-earned and highly valued skills and education of immigrants being well utilized?'

Let us tap into the remarkable wealth of research and results of The Bankwest Curtin Economics Centre, which is an independent economic and social research organisation located within the Curtin Business School at Curtin University, in Western Australia. We are using snippets of key statements and charts from their report *Finding A Place To Call Home* that was released in November 2019. One key clarification to make with regards to the report is this: references to non-English speaking countries refer to countries that do not have English as their native language. For example, Nigeria in Africa would be classified as such, even though English language is the official language in the entire country and the education system is based on English language at all levels – pre-school, primary, secondary and university.

It is glaring that the hard-earned and highly valued skills and education of immigrants are not being well utilized. Beyond the difficult and unfruitful task of finding who to blame for the situation, it is time for immigrants themselves to take the matters of their own success in their hands. This book provides some guidance and hopefully, community leaders will also support the positive change. The sustainable progress that will be achieved will make it easier for the government and their agencies to also enhance the undeniable progress which will be beneficial for all stakeholders. Achieving a match between the potentials of immigrants and the jobs they hold would indeed deliver an extra $6 billion to the economy per year (ref. the BCEC's Report, p49).

48% of immigrants from non English-speaking countries aged 25-64 had a tertiary degree in 2016. Only 36% of immigrants from English-speaking countries and 33% of native-born Australians were tertiary educated.

Nearly 16% of individuals from a non English-speaking country had a postgraduate degree in 2016 while less than 6% of native-born Australians did.

From 2006 to 2016, the number of foreign-born individuals holding a tertiary degree increased by 77%. It increased by only 30% in the native-born population.

Only 60% of migrants from a non English-speaking background are working in well-matched jobs. Potentially, this represents a substantial opportunity cost to the economy from under-utilised skills.

Migrants born outside the main English-speaking countries are more likely to feel their skills are under-utilised compared to migrants from English-speaking countries and native-born workers.

Achieving a perfect match between the educational qualifications of migrants from non English-speaking backgrounds and the jobs they hold could deliver an extra $6 billion to the economy per year.

Opportunities to Utilise the High-Value Skills and Education of Immigrants[8]

Let us refer to the report by the International Federation on Ageing (IFA) for some facts about ageing. This report captured the key outcomes of a meeting of experts and community leaders from diverse ethnic backgrounds to discuss the topic: *Enquiring About Family Caregiving and Their Cultural*

---

[8] Bankwest Curtin Economic Centre, Finding A Place To Call Home. Focus on the States Series, Nov 2019 Pp 38-49

Differences.[9] This meeting was held in Canada and the main relatable findings from this meeting were as follows:

- Data is particularly lacking on the nature of caregiving in culturally and linguistically diverse populations.

- Strong cultural expectations of family care play a significant role in whether or not formal services are accessed. This is viewed as inappropriate for many cultures.

- While there is a strong expectation of family-based care in all cultures, different cultures make different distinctions as to what level of care is considered reasonable and when formal care is requested. Diverse communities are most often the product of immigration, the understanding of culture as it relates to health, illness and caregiving is further complicated by the need to take into account factors related to immigration. These

---

[9] https://ifa.ngo/publication/social-inclusion-and-integration/enquiring-about-family-caregiving-and-their-cultural-differences/

include understanding and response to the meaning and causes of illness, intergenerational tensions arising from mixed generations of families of seniors and younger more acculturated members, and lack of general societal support for strongly held cultural beliefs.

Not all journeys will be the same. Some people would have better experiences than others. Some may call it a bit of luck, others would be more philosophical or spiritual and could refer to their experiences and outcomes as destiny – *it was meant to be*. Thus, not all aspects of the challenges and lessons shared in this book can be generalized across all individuals, cultures and countries in the world. However, some useful insights will be obtained by anyone who reads this book with an open mind to learn from the lived experiences of others. Definitely, the principles are transferable. We all deal with changes in life. The focus of this book relates to those associated with relocation and integrating into a new life and a new country.

3 Change Is About The Only Certainty In Life

Change is inevitable in life. We are confronted with this reality in everyday living. There are different types of changes especially in terms of frequency and impact. We experience some changes daily like waking up from sleep. There are seasonal changes including summer, autumn, winter and spring.

What about the changes accompanying the transition from being single to being married? Literally, this involves two strangers with trails of events, experiences and cultures as part of their upbringings, coming together to live under one roof, share the same bed, same children, same intimacy, etc. If you are reading this book right now, and you have been married for a reasonable period, I reckon that you have had to change a fair bit.

Another set of changes that is worth a mention are those associated with growing from childhood to teenage years, and from the latter to adulthood. Quite a lot of changes are associated with these significant phases of our lives including those related to physical features and mental capacities.

Our professional lives and careers also have their fair share of changes. They include the highs of securing a desired job, the lows of losing one, the feeling of control in a stable job, and the lack of it sometimes during periods of redundancies and layoffs.

There are also changes accompanying ageing, although this is a subject we least want to confront. They include the weakened muscles, the dimmer visions, frequent visits to the restrooms for some cases, and other such similar changes. Ultimately, as humans, we will face the time for dying. This is a change that has some form of finality depending on your faith but does open up another set of changes that dependents and loved ones of the deceased would face.

Now that we have established the prevalence of changes across all walks of life, we now switch to one that adds further dimensions of complexity to those mentioned above. It consists of permanent relocation from one's country of birth and upbringing to another country. This situation could result from emigration, international work transfers, study, expats, family reunions, and the likes. It would typically involve uprooting yourself from familiar terrain, your family, friends and support network to a completely new country to start all over again, many times, not just for a few months or years, but permanently. Providing some guidance to help with navigating this massive change is the main focus of this book. Some preparations before relocation can definitely help.

3.1 Prepare, Prepare, Prepare; But Expect Changes

There are significant benefits for early planning and preparations. This is more than deciding the season for the departure, the type of flight, the choice of stop-overs, and who accompanies you to the airport. It pays to determine your reasons for the big move in the first instance. The value of your *WHYs* must be much more than the opportunity costs i.e. the loss of other alternatives when one alternative is chosen. Indeed, the reasons should be much more compelling than the value of the continuing enjoyment of your family, friends, local network, and the overall comfort zone of your homeland and place of upbringing.

It is very important to foster alignment on this WHY between you and your spouse where applicable. Sometimes it is also necessary to involve other accompanying children or relatives depending on the level of their maturity. Articulating and keeping this refined and alive in you will assist with the process of relocation, settling down and thriving in the new country.

Preparations also require you to research the new country where you will be residing shortly. Knowing that the stay will not be short-term (unless you still retain that option to go back to your country of birth), you will give yourself the best shot at success in the new country if you take the time to know as much as you can well ahead of getting on the flight. Where is the country located? What is the weather like? What languages are spoken there? What is the history like? How about the diversity of people, food and cultures? What is the economy like? What are the biggest supports systems that you can key into?

Consider Australia as an example. We now know that the health industry will keep growing due to the ageing population and growing medical needs. Construction, Sports, Arts and Culture are the other industries with growth potentials. Entrepreneurship and being ready to run your own business is another aspect of economic prosperity and sustainability that should be actively considered during preparations for emigration. Doing this type of preparatory work well ahead of the actual relocation will help you to position yourself better for success.

The reality is that there could never be enough preparations for the significant journey of relocating to reside permanently in a completely new country, including raising families there, securing and sustaining a career over there, and ultimately ageing and dying over there. Expect changes despite commendable preparations. Hopefully, this book will provide you with some information, tips, and tools that will enable you to envisage and plan for these changes, whatever the shape and frequency with which they unravel. Be ready to adopt, to adapt and to achieve even in the face of the changes.

Setting the right goals rightly can increase your chances of success and management of change.

3.2 SMART goals are smart indeed

How SMART are your goals? It is not too early to undertake such self-reflective exercises before relocation. Often, we take this aspect for granted. There should be intentionality in being smart in setting your goals starting from determining your big WHY. This should also be extended to setting goals for other key aspects of life including family, career, and ageing. It could also be useful for health, tourism and education. However, the latter sets of goals are left for other books or programs.

How **specific** are your goals for your family, your career and your ageing before you emigrated and even now? For example, your goal could be to keep your family together and under one roof until the children are grown up and ready to go away to live their own lives. Indeed, separation and divorce are not welcome alternatives in the cultural background of some immigrants. This is not making a case for right or wrong here, it is just what it is. Knowing that they will be relocating to a Western world where the rates are alarmingly high, an immigrant couple could have considered the goal of keeping together as a priority. Goal-setting experts may argue that this could be more specific. For the purpose of this book and the audience, let us take it as specific enough. The same challenges of specificity could also be faced with career and ageing goals.

The difficulty in **measuring** goals for this context is also understandable. However, for the same example of family goals in the previous paragraph, this could be considered as a 2-point measurement - the whole family remaining together is 100% despite the reality that this may not necessarily mean 100% healthy family. The score is 0% for a situation where a child has left home earlier than planned and in an unpleasant fashion, or divorce. Again, it is important to note that this is not being expressed as a failure or blame for anyone in this context. It is about measurement against set goals.

How **achievable** are your goals? Using the same example: is it achievable these days in the Western world to set a goal of keeping a family together? The perception is that it is easier for teenage children to move out of the house. They can be accommodated and even paid some living stipends at short notice via government welfare systems. Again, this cannot be prescriptive. Each individual would have to judge the achievability of their family goals.

The **realistic** aspect of a goal is closely related to the achievable criteria that people sometimes mix them up. But they are different. How realistic is your goal is more related to relevance to your life and purpose. Going back again to the example we have been using for illustration: how important is it to you to keep your family together? This should explain the reason why this may be of higher priority for some people than it is for others.

Setting goals to be **time-bound** is another challenge for many people especially in some life contexts. The timeframe for the example as proposed earlier is really till death separates the last two members of the family – husband and wife. Now, there could be an argument that this should not be the norm. However, this is the context for this book – the assumption that families commenced when the marriage between a man and the wife was consummated with a vow that had the famous and serious line: . . . *till death do us part*. Thus, the expectation is that the couple will traditionally proceed to have children who will grow under their care until they are old enough to move out of the house, and the couple will stick together until death separates them indeed.

On implementation and measurement of outcomes, set goals could be revisited to ensure ongoing SMARTness. Thus, changes should be made for continuous improvement.

> *"I recommend that you focus on both substance and process of your goals. I believe that both are equally important: by setting a high-quality SMART goal you will enable yourself to be conscious and your actions will carry more meaning; meanwhile, it is the execution of the SMART goals strategy that separates achievers from the rest of the people."— Anna Stevens*

The focus now shifts to applying the 'Triple A guide in the context of family, career and ageing for immigrants. Key considerations will be given to the principles and best practices of adoptions and adaptations for achieving set goals. It will also incorporate the impact of sociocultural backgrounds of immigrants and prevailing circumstances in the Western world. Suggestions will be made regarding what to give up, what to adopt, required adjustments, and the need to retain your competitive edge as an immigrant.

4 Adopt Adapt Achieve

To *adopt* simply means to choose or take as one's own. In this book, this means, choosing a new country and life in it as one's own including family life, workplace, aged care system, and other socio-economic aspects. This is particularly relevant for immigrants. Many people challenge the need for any adoption at all. Others have advocated for partial adoption. There are yet some that promote going all the way of full adoption as a requirement to show commitment to the new country. Really, it is not a simple situation to be treated as a right or wrong verdict. If at all, the key points in this book will be situated in a continuum around these arguments. Moreover, every adoption is not an end in itself. Most times, it goes through adaptation of one form or the other to achieve the bigger goals that necessitated the adoption in the first instance.

The other key point is the fact that you do not want to give up everything about your own identity, your cultural backgrounds and your roots. You should not turn yourself entirely into someone different. As the saying goes: *do not try to be someone else, everyone is taken.* You risk losing your unique selling proposition (USP) which gives you your competitive edge in life when you try to be who you are not. Now, it is very difficult to be prescriptive with this point. You know yourself more than anyone else. Take time for self-reflection and self-awareness and turn the information that you unravel into powerful narratives that will sell you better in life including thriving well in your new country of residence. Thus, adopt with wisdom.

To **adapt** is to make suitable to requirements, to adjust or modify to fit. While adoption is generally expected to be done as early as possible on arriving in a new country, adaptation in the context of relocation is envisaged to happen over a length of time. The latter includes adjusting to a new situation which has effects on every area of your life, while still maintaining your purpose and uniqueness. It is also anticipated that there would be ongoing iteration between adoption and adaptation and with frequency and depth that will depend on the individuals involved including their goals, the prevailing circumstances in their lives, external influences in the community, the country and the world. Again, always put your USPs right in the centre of all these considerations.

To *achieve* is to bring to a successful accomplishment of the envisaged purpose. Adoption and adaptation should be intentionally managed towards achieving SMART goals. For immigrants, what was your WHY for making the bold move of emigrating in the first instance? There is one that is very common: taking advantage of the relatively safe and stable socio-economic environments in many countries in the Western world to raise a family. Another one involves seeking "greener pastures" overseas including securing and building a better career that will lead to enough wealth for retirement as well as sharing with other dependents including those that are back in their countries of birth. The need to age and die well is one final example of emigration goals in the context of this book. The latter has unravelled over time as a debate that has caused emotive divides even amongst immigrants. Do you want to age and die in the new country that you now call home or are you planning to go back to your country of birth to end up over there? The author dedicated a section on this *tension of the middle* in his other book "Voices from Home: Wisdom from Our Diasporic Roots."

There is a diversity of goals just as there are different types of people and immigrants. Goals provide targets for effective use of the Triple A model of adoption, adaptation and achievement. They should be SMART as

> *"One part at a time, one day at a time, we can accomplish any goal we set for ourselves."*
> — *Karen Casey*

discussed in Section 3.2 of this book.

There are various aspects of life in which the Triple A guide can be applied in the context of relocation, change and integration. However, the focus of this book is limited to 3 – family, career and ageing. Again, the primary cohorts for the application are members of the immigrant community especially first-generation immigrants. However, the principles and lessons are transferable.

4.1 Family

What is family? It is simply a basic social unit consisting of parents and their children. There is also an extended description as any group of persons closely related by blood, as parents, grandparents, uncles, aunts, nephews, nieces, and cousins. What does family mean to you? How much value do you place on family? What is your dream or goal for your family? Is there alignment on this with your spouse and children (at least the more matured ones)?

First-Generation immigrant parents may have been brought up in a culture with the deep-rooted belief that whilst parents and children are members of the immediate family unit, family narratives also include these extended members. Thus, the original dreams and goals of these first-generation immigrants would have been to keep their beliefs of family to include the extended version even as they now reside in the Western world. This has become more complicated for many immigrant families than anticipated. However, it is never too late to strike a balance.

Fostering alignment on family goals could be a challenging task for immigrant families especially where you have some members of the families that have been born in the Western world – spouses, children for example. There may be divergent views on the definition of marriage, the need to stay together as a family unit despite the odds, respect, disciplinary measures, etc. In one form or the other, immigrants have adopted the prevalent socio-cultural aspects of the new countries where they now call home. Some of the adoptions could be very subtle, but it is happening anyway. Other times, the uptakes are swift and have caused disruptions in families. Often, there is no need to rush into the blame game in such situations when outcomes do not match expectations. It is what it is: while some people keep trying to maintain the culture of their backgrounds and belief systems, others have taken up the new way of living in the belief that *you behave like a Roman when you are in Rome*. This guide proposes the adoption of family life that strikes the right balance in the context of the uniqueness of the immigrant family.

4.1.1 Family Life: How to Adopt your New Country

When people emigrate to live permanently in the Western world, they bring sociocultural practices associated with their backgrounds and upbringings – consciously or not. This is particularly true of first-generation immigrants. These mostly deep-rooted norms will influence how they adopt their new countries of residence as well as how well they integrate. Realistically, which of these practices should be dropped off? Which of them should be retained? Moreover, *old habits die hard*. Some of the socio-cultural practices to be used for further illustration are patriarchy, respect, greetings and names, disciplinary measures for children, visitation and personal spaces, and caring for elderly folks.

Patriarchy

Patriarchy is a social system in which men hold primary power and predominate in roles of political leadership, moral authority, social privilege and control of property (www.wikipedia.org). Most contemporary societies practice the system in one form or the other even if this may not be explicitly included as part of their constitutions and laws. However, it is known to be the more visible tradition in many countries in places like Africa, Asia and The Middle East. It is largely perceived as a system where men have control over their wives and children.

Just the mention of the word *patriarchy* in some social contexts in the west could trigger significant and emotional backlash as it is largely branded as a vehicle for oppression and domination of women. It would be too hasty to pronounce the system as bad or evil in the context of this book and particularly in the spirit of multiculturalism. It could be argued that many cultures have thrived well with such a system. It is meant to ensure that there is orderliness especially in the home, they would claim. Of course, some men and cultures have taken the "control factor" to the extreme to actually dominate, cause fear, and perpetuate domestic violence in the home with significant consequences. Unfortunately, people that have grown up in such cultures may not have considered the system to be wrong even when done wrongly. It was the generational norm for them.

The situation is different in most parts of the Western world, especially in the current dispensation. Unfortunately, some immigrants from such backgrounds where patriarchy was the norm may only find out the hard way - when much damage has been done. The visibility of progress in ensuring equal rights across gender is undeniable. Women are encouraged and supported to exercise their choices not to be mistreated, and rightly so. Everyone should feel safe around their fellow humans irrespective of gender and especially within the family unit. It is an offence to commit domestic violence in the west and this could be punishable by a jail sentence. Offenders cannot hide behind the "cover" of *this is family matters, mind your business*.

However, there are still significant rates of marital breakdowns in families in the west as we saw from the ABS charts in Section 2. Moreover, the rates of these breakdowns in marriages involving immigrants are almost at the same level as those of non-immigrants. The increasing number of incidences of family domestic violence and homicides among immigrant families further indicates the need for more efforts at finding a solution especially if there could be a correlation between these unpleasant events and relocating to the west. Would immigrant couples have divorced or even engaged in this other worse malaise if they were still back in their places of birth? Of course, there is the other side of the story that if such correlation exists, it could prove the reality of suppression of the rights of women in many of the places of birth of these immigrants. Irrespective of which side of the arguments wins, the question of whether there could still be some value for the "right" patriarchy as a possible solution for sustainable relocation for some ethnic groups. Indeed, any practice that promotes mistreatment of women should not be acceptable under any culture and jurisdiction. Maybe this is why matriarchy is also being practised for some kind of balance, just a thought. A healthy debate will allow all options to be brought into the mix. In reality, many immigrants were brought up in some form of patriarchy and they claim that there are beneficial aspects of the culture.

Should patriarchy that promotes equality, leadership, protection, and orderliness in families be considered as a viable option for adoption? Is it reasonable to expect that immigrants will not just disown such a system under which they have arguably thrived well before relocating? For example, could there be value in the belief system that promotes respect for elders in ethnic communities including opportunities to bring issues for them to resolve based on their wisdom rather than running to the relatively more expensive options of court proceedings? Of course, it will be vital to ensure that such a system does not become a protective mechanism for abuse and violence. Another alternative could be a hybrid system where such ethnocultural practices support the established legal jurisdictions with the latter taking precedence where there are conflicts in the application. These are just some thoughts for considerations by law and policymakers of countries with an increasing population of ethnic groups that may be suitable for such pilots. It has to work for the overall good of the entire community, ultimately.

Respect, Greetings and Family Names

Respect within the family is generally a big factor in the cultures of many immigrants especially those from collectivist backgrounds like many African and Asian countries. For example, it is disrespectful to call an older person by his or her first name when trying to get their attention or even just expressing pleasantries. It is also the norm that children would say some form of greetings to parents or older folks when they come across them before expecting to be greeted in reply. The reverse is almost a taboo and could trigger the fear of a curse being brought on the child for non-compliance. Retaining family names over generations is another cultural practice for many immigrants. It is common to find the same surname surviving many generations.

The situation is increasingly different in the Western world. Greetings are not so regimented. Older folks are generally called by their first names particularly outside the immediate family circle of dad, mum, uncle, aunty. There seems to be less effort to retain family names over generations. Indeed, it is progressively more challenging to force children of immigrants who are born in the Western world to continue with the sociocultural norms described in the previous paragraph despite the efforts of persistent parents.

Over time, many immigrants have begun to adopt the prevailing family culture in the Western world. Most times, these are done subconsciously. *When you live in Rome, you begin to behave like a Roman indeed.* We do not seem to struggle any longer in calling older folks by their names. However, it is still hard to do the same within the immigrant community. For example, in a typical African community, we end up with some form of hybrids like adding "oga," "uncle," "aunty," "mr," "daddy," "mummy" before the names just to still try and retain some respect. There have been cases where children of immigrants born in the Western world have revolted when instructed to call older folks "uncle" or "aunty" etc. "They are not my uncle or aunt," they would argue. Many parents are beginning to empathise with them.

Indeed, parents seem to be more accepting of the reality that placing the burden of full compliance on the shoulders of their children is not only unreasonable, but it could also end up being counter-productive. After all, the Western world is the only world these children know. They hardly know the world of their parents' cultural backgrounds. The once-in-a-decade visits to the country of birth of their parents will never match the world they have always known and will continue to know, going forward.

The aspect of retaining family names seems to be one that has been relatively easier for immigrants to adjust to. Many families in these cultural backgrounds have been observed to be flexible in adopting the culture of placing less importance on the need to continue in the same family names that have been passed down from generations. Children of First Generation immigrants have taken up the first names of their Father and that means that Family name dies out with that generation. These are choices that are being made in the contexts of individual families.

Disciplinary Measures for Children

Disciplinary measures for children is another aspect that has divided communities in the past as many older folks even those that have lived all their lives in the Western world struggled to come to terms with having to adopt the new culture where physical discipline of children like using a light stick to beat the hand or even smacking on the buttocks is now generally prohibited.

This has been particularly challenging for immigrant families especially first-generation immigrants that relocated at adult age. They have been brought up with various types and degrees of such physical disciplinary measures. Many of them do believe, right or wrongly, that they have turned out better as a result. One argument that has been made for this option is related to the principles of positive and negative reinforcements. Praising or rewarding a child's positive behaviour will likely reinforce the repeat of that behaviour in the future. The reverse is also true as per supporters of such strict disciplinary style: "punishing" a child for negative behaviour will likely make the child desist from similar behaviour in the future on recollecting the consequence if he or she proceeds with such behavior. Unfortunately, there were occasions where such actions caused physical injuries on the child. Now we know that other less visible injuries could have been left on the child including fear, low esteem, etc.

It is illegal in many parts of the Western world to leave an injury on a child however justifiable even from action by parents trying to instil discipline on their children. Many times, the injury could have resulted from unplanned actions like carrying out the disciplinary action in rage. The system in the west is swift in response to a report of such injuries especially when it comes to minors (mostly children under 18 years). The allegation could be quickly escalated as child abuse or domestic violence causing bodily harm. Children cannot fight for themselves hence the state fights for them, and such fights are taken seriously most times. There have been cases where immigrant parents have gone to jail for such actions however well-intentioned. Parents generally love their children but love does not provide a reasonable argument before the law when it comes to how you discipline your children in the Western world.

Some may argue that the outcomes of succumbing to such a system in the west have not been so good for their families. The rates at which immigrant children are involved in crimes and being jailed (refer to the ABS statistics in Section 2) could provide justification for their frustrations. While there should be no debate about the need for everyone to be subject to the same law, could there be some form of culturally appropriate support that may be necessary for some groups? What about the feelings of failure for parents as they would still take responsibility for such unpleasant outcomes for their children. They claim that they could not perform their roles of being able to discipline their children the way they have been brought up themselves. Of course, they would have justified the preference because it worked for them, they would further claim.

Sometimes the situations with parents' disciplinary measures for their children in the Western world do not lend themselves to simplistic solutions. This becomes even more challenging in the context of achieving set goals. Let us go back to the example of family goal we have been using for our illustration: *keeping the family together under one roof until the children grow more matured and they leave home to continue their own respective lives as adults*. A strict disciplinary system in the home may likely cause a child to explore escape mechanisms to get out of the home much earlier than anticipated. It is easier in the Western world in terms of the provisions in the welfare system for financial and social services support to young children in such contexts. Thus, each family, and particularly parents, would need to consider the impact of losing a child to the outside world where the exposure to negative influences could be higher. Compare the latter to a situation where you scale back your disciplinary measures to merely using your voice and "negotiating" restraints and boundaries with your children. Arguably, this may mean upbringing of children in the west with dissimilar discipline and character that their first-generation immigrant parents had in their own upbringing. Which preferable if allowed to make a choice? But the reality is that these are two different worlds and that needs to be considered as well as differences in individual family circumstances.

Visitations & Personal Spaces

The visitation culture in the west is another interesting consideration regarding changes that immigrants would need to confront as part of settling and living in the Western world. Immigrants especially those from collectivist backgrounds have typically grown up in communal settings where people can pay you a visit, unannounced. Thus, the person or family being visited will, to their discomfort, quickly adjust and "gladly" welcome the visitor. It is particularly important and face-saving that you receive and welcome visitors anytime especially if they are part of the extended family.

This is not the case in most parts of the Western world where it is a prevalent practice to acknowledge the personal spaces of people including family members. For example, one cannot just appear on the doorstep of another person or family to visit. It is advisable to call, check if they will be available, and book an appointment (even if you do not use that exact term). Your intending host will confirm a suitable date and time. One of the logical explanations for this practice is that people are busy with work, shifts, family time, and other essentials. They need space and time to fit in anything that is not part of the routine. This is normal for the Westerners that have lived like this all their lives. They like their spaces which is the individualistic culture of the west. Immigrants require adjustments over time.

Remarkably, many immigrants seem to have adopted this culture of the west over time. Many are now comfortable in keeping to themselves except for friends and families with long-standing relationships. Again, there could be a valid case for finding the balance that works for more immigrants more of the time. Loneliness and all the associated social and mental issues are widely discussed as a challenge with such an individualistic lifestyle. There have been a few reports of people that have been dead for days and even weeks before their bodies were discovered. Such situations could be prevented or at least the damage mitigated by a culture that promotes communal living and togetherness which are the hallmarks of collectivist cultures. Indeed, there are some competitive advantages in preserving, practising and sharing this culture while living in the Western world.

Many of the cultural practices associated with the upbringing of first-generation immigrants are not working in the Western world where they now call home. There have been adjustments as they adopt a mix of practices already in them as part of their upbringing with those that are prevalent in their new countries of residence. To continue to stick strictly to the old has caused lots of tensions in immigrant families especially during the early settlement period. This could derail them from the path to achieving their set goals. Ongoing adaptations would be required for the sustainability of immigrant families and their future generations in the Western world.

4.1.2 Adapt or you could become extinct!

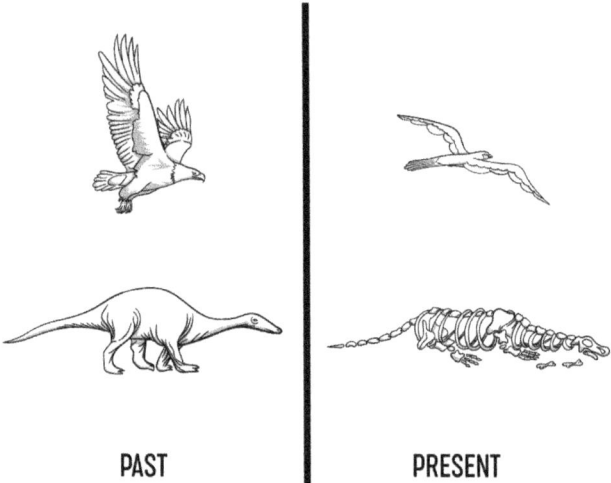

PAST | PRESENT

IT IS NOT THE STRONGEST OF THE SPECIES THAT SURVIVES, NOR THE
MOST INTELLIGENT. IT IS THE ONE THAT IS MOST ADAPTABLE TO CHANGE.

CHARLES DARWIN - SCIENTIST

Old habits die hard as we know. People are often reluctant to change their ways of doing things, especially things they have been doing for a long time. It is even worse if they have been seemingly successful doing them. Immigrants can learn from the story of the dinosaur and the bird during the ancient era. The dinosaur did not change despite the changing times. They were so confident that they can keep moving around, eating, and living the way they had always lived over the years. Unfortunately, they died off over time and became extinct so that you do not see dinosaurs again in this current era. The birds, on the other hand embraced change, they proactively and quickly adapted to the prevailing environmental factors over time. They learnt and made changes, however small, along the way. They tried to change fast. Despite failures along the way, they also learned fast. They did not only survive over time, but they also got better and slicker based on their responses to changes. They experienced the same prevailing environmental conditions. While the dinosaurs died off, the birds survived, they improved, they grew and they multiplied.

The sociocultural systems and styles for families that formed the upbringing of many immigrants did work very well in the past and back in their places of births and homelands. Some of the examples presented earlier include patriarchy, strict disciplinary measures for children, manners of expressing respect, greetings and preservation of family names, and finally, communal living. However, many of them will not work in the new countries of residence. Moreover, there are already sociocultural practices in these countries that have made room for newcomers. Why would they change all of a sudden? Thus immigrants will naturally adopt mixtures of these practices as part of their settlement process.

Immigrants will naturally continue with some of their native cultural practices in their pure states when they newly arrive. Over time, some parts will be dropped off while they adopt some of the cultures of the new countries. In most cases, they will continue with a blend of some sort between cultures from their roots and those already established in the new places. This adoption process will typically continue for the settlement period with their goals in mind. Thereafter, immigrants will continuously adapt to be fit for purpose based on the ever-changing prevailing conditions and the need to achieve set family goals. Whether the immigrant fails like the dinosaur or succeeds like the bird will depend on his or her proactive stances and adaptability to changes.

Immigrants need adjustment with regards to patriarchy, disciplinary measures, demand for special respect and greetings, and holding on to family names. Hanging on to what we have always known and the system of our own upbringing does not work, at least over a long time. Men particularly need to shift. The rights of women and children are so real and visible that no one can miss it unless they choose to. There are even feelings in many immigrant communities (of course, men mostly), that the law is too weighted to the rights of women and children that this takes away the manhood that has largely been the signature of the cultural backgrounds in these communities. That is a big trigger for change! Even religious inclination seems to matter less in this context. Some people will either continue with the old mindset of strict adherence without making necessary changes like the dinosaur. They may end up being frustrated, stressed, and some may fall sick, and even die. The world will move on.

It is difficult to prescribe an exact type and degree of adaptation as families are different even within immigrants from the same country and the same ethnic community. However, here are some thoughts. Find the right position in the continuum that works for you, your family, and which aligns with the law in your new country. This also requires that you find the right information to help you reposition yourself better in the context of your set goals, and of course, with the welfare of the entire family in mind.

Patriarchy seems to be a term that does not trigger positive vibes in the Western world. However, one can display the good parts of the system without necessarily being called a patriarch. Provide leadership for your family as much as you reasonably can. Be the one that will always step back and consider the big picture of your family goals however tense the situation may be in the family. Learn to partner with your family especially your wife. This is one aspect that would require many immigrant men to do some more work. However, it is a vital adjustment if you want to survive and thrive as a family in the Western world. We must also tap into our wealth of wisdom in leading our children as well. There is a need to shift from the expectation that children will stand still and listen when parents speak. Learn the act of balancing firmness with negotiation to have reasonably good outcomes for everyone, ultimately. The requirement for adjustments is heightened by the prevalence of the internet, social media, video games, peer influences, etc. Leaders keep the big picture in mind.

With the aspects of respect, greetings and family names, parents should keep reminding their children to honour the culture of their heritage. Regularly exposing them to the culture can be helpful. This will include speaking the language and demonstrating these behaviours at home, where you can. It would also be helpful to undertake regular trips to your home country for face to face interactions with other members of your family tree. The alternative is the use of technology - telephone, Skype, WhatsApp, face time, and other appropriate platforms.

Adjusting to the situation of respect from children is one aspect of change and integration in the new country that will be challenging especially if your children are being raised in the Western world with little or no rootedness in your own cultural background.

> *"Do not let what you cannot do interfere with what you can do."*
> *— John Wooden*

Once again, keep your eyes on the bigger picture of your family goals. You may eventually have to greet your children first, treat them like another adult (especially teenagers), and you may accept the reality that your family name may not survive beyond the second generation. Gather in more gains and count your few losses, and like the bird, adapt and keep flying.

Immigrants require adaptation regarding disciplinary measures for children indeed. There are many substitutes to physical discipline. Parents can verbally caution their children. They can also use the appropriate tone of voice to convey their messages of disapproval to their children as the case may deserve. There is also the option of withdrawal of privileges where appropriate. Use of timeouts is another one that may be suitable for younger children. There are no physical aspects in all these cases. The best practice is to do these in love and ensure reasonableness in terms of timing and depth of the actions. Whatever disciplinary measure, try to ensure that it is done in such a way that it does not come across to the children as an attempt to shame them. Strike the right balance with discipline and rewards. Do the latter more than the former even if this forces you as a parent to find more occasions and events to praise/reward than those that require enforcing discipline. Use your words! After all, there's still power in your mouth, tone and body language. Don't allow these to be drowned out by the prevalent culture in your new country. The lives of your children and families matter a lot.

Going back to their country of birth and upbringing could be one option for immigrants. This will be particularly appropriate for you as an individual if you know yourself that you have judged that you are not likely to change despite the points presented so far in this book. Indeed, that could

> *"I can't change the direction of the wind, but I can adjust my sails to always reach my destination." — Jimmy Dean*

be a better option than put yourself and possibly your love ones through all the stress and pains of infighting in the family. Nevertheless, be prepared for the possibility that your family may not go back with you especially if they are now citizens of the new country of your residence. Adaptation is still your best shot at achieving your goals.

4.1.3 Achieve your family goals!

To achieve a goal is to bring things to a successful end or to accomplish the envisaged purpose. Considering our sample family goal that has been used for illustration in this book: *keeping the family together under one roof until the children grow more matured and they leave home to continue their own respective lives as adults and until parents are separated by death.*

How is this goal being achieved for immigrants that have taken up permanent residency in the Western world? We saw the statistics of divorce rates in Australia as a case study earlier on in Section 2. It indicates that there are so many divorces involving couples and members of immigrant communities. Of course, the aim of bringing this up in this book is not to prejudge anyone that has gone through (or still going through) the painful experience of divorce.

> *"You just can't beat the person who never gives up."*
> — *Babe Ruth*

Indeed, it is commendable that people do bounce back and still achieve their family goals despite such significant challenges along the way.

Nevertheless, our main focus is in the context of the set goals for family life in the Western world is that people prefer to keep their families together in love, strength and growth. After all, many immigrants made the bold move of relocating to the Western world with the hope of better economic lives for themselves and their families - together. It is most likely that less thought was given to the challenges they will face in terms of family life and associated culture clashes between what they knew and what they have met in their new countries of residence.

Immigrants should keep their eyes on their family goal of keeping everyone together as much as reasonably practicable. Parents can lead the children in a regular exercise to acknowledge cultural practices that have been adopted and the impacts on the family goals. They can also

> *"Believe you can and you're halfway there."*
> *— Theodore Roosevelt*

reflect on prevailing changes and the need for adaptation to keep achieving their goals. It is important to keep that feedback loop going. Revisit sociocultural practices to drop off, identify others to pick up, and maintain the right balance. Evolve and get better at doing family like the bird rather than remaining inflexible and dying off like the dinosaur.

4.2 Career

Career is another aspect of life that immigrants would need to consider applying the Triple A model. Just like the family experiences discussed in the previous sections, they would need to go through some form of adoption, adaptation and achievement loop in the contexts of the professional and sociocultural norms in the new countries of residence. The specific case for this book is moving from a less advanced country to the Western world.

Various industries and professions have their ways of doing things in their respective domains. There are also additional layers of cultural norms and nuances associated with them while operating in different countries and regions of the world. Consider cases of immigrants that have relocated to Australia after many years of working as project managers in the oil and gas industry in Africa. Why would they experience challenges in fitting in right away in the same industry and profession in Australia? Why is it so common that many of them end up in jobs that they had not envisaged for themselves and their careers? After all, it is the same project management processes, same professional language, same oil and gas value chain, same typical organizational structure especially in terms of disciplines and teams required to achieve similar project outcomes. It comes down to differences in sociocultural norms, nuances, unspoken rules etc. that are unique to each country, over and beyond the generic industry, professional and technical boundaries.

A quick caution on the risk of generalization: Some immigrants have relocated from job to job with little or no delay in securing the employment of their choices. However, in the continuum of immigrants that end up in the exact careers of their choices and those that settle for the ones that they least preferred, there will be more clusters around the latter end than

> *"You never achieve success unless you like what you are doing."*
> — Dale Carnegie

the former. Thankfully, the principles of the Triple A guide in this book are applicable for all enthusiasts and learners that are interested in the lived experiences and best practices of how immigrants navigate the terrain of employment and career pursuits in their new countries of residence.

Similar to the family context, many immigrants had career goals even before they left their countries of birth. They may not have documented them (and they should), but they had goals anyway. More often, it is about relocating and securing a great job in the new country and then growing on the job to build a remarkable career. Commonly, it is about generating enough income to take care of families (both immediate and extended) and create significant savings for a good life after retirement.

However, the reality becomes a bit more evident when you start realizing that your folders (physical or email inbox) are getting fuller with those letters informing you that you are not successful in being invited for an interview, in the interview itself, or in securing the job. The scope of this book does not cover the different phases of experiences and emotions that an immigrant typically goes through during these weeks, months or even years of receiving such negative feedback. You may find some anecdotal experiences in the other book by the author: *A Handbook for Migrants: The Good, The Challenges and The Lessons.*

It will suffice at least to mention that the loss of esteem, the need for cash flow (especially for the breadwinner of a family), and the positive aspect of resilience, will drive the immigrant to explore the option of picking up a 'survival job' while hoping for a breakthrough in securing their preferred job in which they have the qualifications, training and many times, previous experiences. Others also venture into further studies with the hope that locally acquired certificates or degrees will open the right doors for them. While knowledge is not wasted, many do not achieve the aim for the pursuit of such additional qualification – they still could not secure employment of choice. This situation is further confirmed in the research by Bankwest Curtin Economic Centre (BCEC).

35% of recent immigrants have pursued further studies after arriving in the country.	A quarter of immigrants who already had a postgraduate degree on arrival completed another postgraduate degree in Australia.	We estimate that in 2017, there were 715,000 migrants from a non English-speaking background with more years of education than is normally required for their job.

Immigrants are Studying and Adding more Qualifications[10]

Does additional academic qualification enhance the immigrant's chance of securing a job or career progression? Could there be a more value-adding way of acquiring the required skills?

This Triple A guide and the principles therein could be useful in further facilitating more successes. But first, let us consider and set a sample goal for illustration of how the model will work for immigrants. Note, however, that this goal represents the reality on ground as per the working experiences of the author in his interactions with immigrants and

---

[10] Bankwest Curtin Economic Centre, Finding A Place To Call Home. Focus on the States Series, Nov 2019 Pp 38-49

other key stakeholders in the professional, corporate, and community sectors – especially multicultural Australia as a case study.

> *To secure a role in my career of choice within the first six months of relocation which will help generate enough income to care for myself, my family, and still have enough savings at retirement for a high-end lifestyle post-retirement.*

4.2.1 Are your Career Goals SMART?

Now that we acknowledge the importance of a SMART goal (see Section 3.2), let us analyze the sample career goal as a mini exercise and illustration. It is specific enough: secure a job as per career of choice. It is measurable: he or she secures the job or not. Is it achievable? Yes, it is! However few, some immigrants do achieve this goal. Is this goal relevant? This is one that is personal just like the family situation. However, there are some considerations involved. What is the impact on your life and purpose if this goal is not achieved? How much do you need to secure a job in your career of choice? How much weight do you place on this compared to continuing on a survival job? How do you feel with the increasing reality of hard-earned qualifications just going obsolete over time from lack of use? What about the impact on your esteem? Which job will generate enough income for your family upkeep and savings for living a good lifestyle at retirement? Finally, the goal has a timeframe – 6 months.

The immigrant that invests some time and efforts (and possibly professional support) in undertaking this exercise will more likely have a good shot at achieving the goals. Complacency does not help in any form. Indeed, there are probing questions to unravel in the context of historical experiences and prevalent contexts. It is helpful to identify and articulate gaps and actions for bridging them. It is common for intending and new immigrants to be told (via body or verbal languages): "This is how it is here, get a survival job! After all, you need to care for your family, you need to pay your bills," etc.

Thus, should a highly qualified immigrant engineer, who has had many years of relevant work experience and a fulfilling career before relocation, insist on continuing to seek for a job at that level? How relevant is such a stance to him or her? How long is it reasonable to continue without a job and to live on welfare support? Anyway, most governments in the Western world are becoming stricter in providing welfare to newcomers. In some instances, they will make you do the unwanted "survival jobs" for the welfare payment anyway. This is called *working for the dole* in Australia. Thus, the earlier immigrants can get unto the pathway of sustainably achieving their career goals, the better for all stakeholders especially themselves. SWOT analysis may further assist in contextualizing and enhancing the development and achievement of your SMART goals that will work for you.

4.2.2 Do you need SWOT Analysis for your Career?

SWOT is an acronym for strengths, weaknesses, opportunities, and threats. As a strategic planning technique, it can be applied to your career to help you achieve your goals. While your strengths and weakness are frequently internally-related, opportunities and threats are mostly focused on the external environment. Here is a version of SWOT descriptions:

- Strengths are the characteristics of your career that give you an advantage over others.

- Weaknesses are the characteristics of your career that put you at a disadvantage relative to others.

- Opportunities are factors in the environment of your career that you could exploit to its advantage.

- Threats are factors in the environment that could cause trouble for your career.

The degree to which the internal environment matches with the external environment is generally a reasonably good predictor of a strategic fit and sustainability for your career. Properly conducting this process will help you to identify these SWOTs which could further enable you to unleash your potentials in the right direction of achieving your career goals.

The other point to acknowledge is that what could be your 'SWOT' while working in your country of birth may not necessarily be the same on relocating to live and work in a new country. Thus a SWOT analysis of your career would consist of determining all these aspects – your strengths, weakness, opportunities, and threats based on self-awareness, deep reflections, thorough research, and fact findings. The exercise should be performed at key points in your career progress and when you experience significant changes including relocating to a new industry, new team, new profession, etc. It should be done with utmost sincerity as the outcomes would form the firm foundation for building your career going forward. You do not want to build on a lie which is a shaky foundation and which may eventually crumble with time, and strong environmental elements, usually associated with career pathways.

In the context of this book: SWOT analysis should be done specifically as part of your preparations for the big move of relocating to a new country. This would need you to undertake some self-reflection to articulate the internal characteristics and research, for external factors that will provide you with a good view of the journey ahead regarding your career. However, it is never too late even if you have relocated already and have now been living in the country for a while. After all, we all need to reinvent, reset or recharge our careers now and then.

We will now use a case for illustrating the power combination of SMART goals and SWOT analysis as we further demonstrate the value of the Triple A guide. An experienced project manager is currently working on a construction project at a closing phase in his home country in Africa. He is 37 years old. He has just received a confirmation email that his skilled migration visa application is successful and he would need to arrive in Australia within the next few months on permanent residency status. Along with his wife and one child, they would now make arrangements to relocate shortly. Within a relatively short time, he came up with his initial draft of his career goal in relocating and permanently living in Australia:

To secure a role as a project manager within the first six months of relocation which will help generate enough income to care for me, my family, and savings at retirement for maintaining a high standard lifestyle post-retirement.

4.2.3 Career: How to Adopt your new country

Relocating to a new country is challenging in itself already. Adding the extra dimensions of dealing with changes in career transitioning could become quite overwhelming for some folks. There are uncertainties in securing a job as well as keeping one. Industries and professions are the same across the globe. For example, the building and construction industry and the processes involved will be the same whether in Africa or Australia. It is a similar situation with the project management profession. Then why is it that an experienced project manager in the building industry in Africa that uses the same international code of standards cannot secure a job right away in Australia on relocation? This is the situation even when there are numerous advertised vacancies. There are no one-answer-fit-all-situations with this complex scenario. However, there could be some explanations in differences in economic, social, and cultural norms.

Let us demonstrate the application of the Triple A guide for this case study based on SWOT analysis and mapping. The sequence for this book is Opportunities, Strengths, Weaknesses and Threats. While the objective is to propose an Adopt strategy that provides the best chance for success in a career in the new location, a comparison with the previous location will also provide some valuable references and inputs. After all, one's history and self-awareness can provide great lessons and guide for better positioning for the future as long as one is willing to learn and make necessary adjustments. Recall that Australia is the new country for the case study. However, the principles and lessons are typical for most countries with immigration as a policy for development and growth. Some emphases are also placed on skilled migrant professionals and again, with applicability for other immigrants via pathways of family reunion, humanitarian, business etc. Overall, the Triple A guide can be contextualised for different countries and careers.

Opportunities – factors in the environment that could be exploited for your career

Stable economy / World-Class Infrastructure / High Standard of Living	Remarks and Guidance on how to Adopt
Australia offers a stable economy and high standard of living like many countries in the Western world. There is strong fiscal discipline and governance at all levels of government. There are pipelines of ongoing and scheduled projects despite intermittent global economic uncertainties. Other attractive factors relate to the quality of life including dependable and affordable medical care, world-class transportation system, education, welfare, and security.	Stable economy, world-class infrastructure and high standard of living are some of the reasons (*the WHYs*) for people to emigrate even when they have reasonably good jobs back in their homelands. They consider longer-term prospects, overall stability and security for themselves and their families.
Most of these enablers are lacking in many home countries of immigrants including those in the region of Africa. Lack of fiscal discipline and prevalent corrupt practices have caused so much uncertainty in the system that even when the prospects for projects are evident, these other underlying factors have been known to constitute barriers for progress. However, immigrants have opportunities back in their homelands that they could tap into while living in the west. They have the edge in harnessing these opportunities.	Immigrants should adopt these undeniable benefits while also exploring opportunities back in their homelands. They can be the 'bridge' between investors and employers in the west and opportunities back in their homelands. They can exploit the advantages of knowing and living in multiple worlds.

Strengths - characteristics of your career that give you an advantage over others

Strengths	Remarks and Guidance on how to Adopt
Immigrants bring so much strength to their new countries of residence in the aspect of careers. They bring skills and value to businesses. It is widely acknowledged that cultural diversity contributes to creativity in the workplace. Hopefully, employers, leaders and team members recognize, celebrate and give credit accordingly. Recent data have shown that some organisations would have to look beyond the Western world for new opportunities to remain viable. Thus, proactive immigrants are the best candidates that these companies would need for bridging these gaps. Immigrants are mostly multinational, multicultural, and resilient. They know the terrains in and around their homelands, countries of birth and upbringing. They may not necessarily have the high-worth networks for businesses, but they present as the best candidates for resilience. After all, it was their backyards! Arts and culture industries are another set of areas with opportunities that immigrants could present as a very competitive candidate for jobs and investments facilitators.	The strengths that immigrants bring into their new countries are needful and undeniable. Articulate yours as an immigrant! Build, refine, and stretch them as required. You can also propose to employers the options of exploring opportunities back in your homeland even where they were not initially interested. Be proactive by developing key leads before relocation and maintain them as you settle into your new places. They could help your career.

A continuous mass exodus of skilled professionals "brain drain" to the Western world is predicted to continue as long as there is no significant shift in the economic and social stability of the migrant's homeland. Indeed, why would newcomers not gladly adopt these inherent opportunities in their new countries? Realistically, people would prefer to relocate to countries with high standard and sustainable infrastructural and economic prosperity – not just for themselves, but also their families.

The Weaknesses section of SWOT will be briefly presented under 4 key areas that have been known to greatly influence how well immigrants settle and thrive in their professional callings. You can read an extended version in the author's other book: *A Handbook for Migrants: The Good, The Challenges and The Lessons*. They are (1) language and communication, (2) academic and professional qualifications, (3) work experiences, and (4) networking. These are not the only factors that could give you an edge or become a barrier. However, they largely contribute to how soon and how well immigrants can secure and sustain their employment of choice in the Western world. Again, we will use our case study for illustration but this time, the immigrants have arrived and started living in the new country for a few months already. They are getting to know their way around.

Weaknesses - characteristics that put you at a disadvantage relative to others

(1)Language and Communication	Remarks and Guidance on how to Adopt
Limited English language skills are particularly challenging for immigrants from non-English speaking countries. They would need to spend months to learn to speak, read and write in English. The family in our case study came from a country in Africa where English is the official language. But the reality is that they will still be classified as non-English speaking since English is not the native language in their home country. There are also cases where locals cannot readily understand immigrants even when they genuinely want to engage. Communication styles, accents, voice tones, body language, etc., are different in many instances. Logically, people would prefer friendships and teams where they can understand one another. This becomes a weakness for new and emerging immigrants regarding securing new employment or retaining current ones. It could also constitute barriers to career progression. The barriers are more evident in jobs like teaching, office reception, call centres etc. with more verbal engagement. The reverse is also frustrating when immigrants cannot understand colleagues and locals. But the action to learn to communicate better is more on the former than the latter.	There are no easy solutions for language and communication barriers. Immigrants would have to adopt applicable languages. This may require learning, practising and communicating in the language until mastery. Many immigration departments now mandate pass of English tests as a requirement for residency visas. The other aspects like differences in accent and voice tone will mostly get better with time. Immigrants should mix-up with locals as much as reasonably practicable as part of the settlement process.

(2) Academic and professional qualifications	Remarks and Guidance on how to Adopt
The lack of recognition of hard-earned qualifications is another barrier to consider. Certificates of immigrants are being made redundant causing them to be 'flushed down the drain' at an alarming rate. This is irrespective of the fact that these qualifications would have been reviewed and verified by relevant Australian professional bodies as part of the skilled migration process, where applicable. Many employers in the Western world place more weight on practical work experiences than academic qualifications. This is the case for Australia. Even in roles where academic qualifications are typically required like lecturing or researching in the universities or teaching in schools, they would value qualifications that are earned locally than those from overseas. Some potential employers will request checks via professional bodies. The feedback reports are typical as follows: (1) the overseas qualification meets the requirements. (2) It does not meet the requirement and cannot be used. (3) It partially meets the requirement and further actions specified - mostly additional bridging study. Consequently, many immigrants have not used their qualifications for work.	For intending, new and emerging immigrants: Firstly, accept the reality that there is no guarantee that you will use your qualifications even as a skilled visa holder. Secondly, be willing to be flexible including acquiring relevant short courses that may eventually secure a job for you. Lastly, ensure you are informed about the qualifications of demand well ahead of your arrival. Check the Country's approved list of skilled occupations as they change regularly. Be flexible and fill the gaps even while you are working survival jobs in the meantime. Never give up on your goals even if it takes a few more steps to achieve them.

(3) Work experiences	Remarks and Guidance on how to Adopt
Immigrants face a dilemma when it comes to the challenges with local work experience as a requirement for employment. This can be likened to the classic chicken and egg analogy: how do you acquire this experience without employment? They end up missing out for many years as they struggle to secure opportunities with local companies that will give them a chance. Previous work experiences are sometimes relegated by potential employers. The common reasons are that these non-local experiences are not compliant with local systems and/or they cannot be validated. While this is understandable for some disciplines and industries like law, defence, immigration, etc., but many times, normal logic is not adhered to. One would have thought that engineering skills and experiences in an industry like mining will be mostly transferable. The other factor that causes a lot of frustration is the fact that this situation is not due to lack of efforts on the part of the newcomer. It is common to have highly qualified immigrants giving accounts of how they have applied for job opportunities in the hundreds without success. This weakens the zest for career progression and contributing to the economic growth of their new country.	This situation with work experience is the reality on ground in most countries in the west. Arguably, governments and employing organisations have their pre-set strategies and demands in terms of the regions they want the newcomers to relocate to, industries & professions they want them to work in, types of training and qualifications required. Immigrants can be proactive in accessing this information and being guided accordingly. This will help during preparation for the relocation, and targeting work and volunteering experiences.

(4)Professional Network	Remarks and Guidance on how to Adopt
Employers and hiring managers want employees that would fit into the team and help them to succeed. Thus they depend on interviews and references for a feel of the candidates that will most closely fit the 'person' on their minds. How often would a new immigrant stand the chance? What about the situations with names? Compare 'John' to 'Uwangatugugaga.' Even if many immigrants do not have names as complex, but it is common for them to attach much importance to names and associated cultural affiliations. However, this could become a source of weakness in competing for scarce employment opportunities. How many current and potential hiring managers would an immigrant know? How many of these managers will know enough of the potentials in immigrants to look beyond the differences in race, names, accents and other external features? The reality is that new and emerging immigrants do not have as much professional network that will lead to many potential job opportunities and employers. It takes time to build such a network after the relocation. The saying *your network is your net-worth* also applies to careers. Unfortunately, this is one asset that many immigrants do not have on relocation.	For new and emerging immigrants: Get out of your comfort zones to meet people and preferably, more locals, strangers and not just staying around people like you. The earlier this is done, the better. Thankfully, the act of networking can be learnt and mastered. Be open-minded and try not to prejudge, the most viable help could come from unexpected quarters. Display hunger for success and achievements. Be authentic and positive when you talk about your story. Take time to select and put forward your best references for job applications.

Threats - factors in the environment that could cause trouble for your career

Threats	Remarks and Guidance on how to Adopt
This would be presented for 3 different contexts – one's personal life, the workplace, and the global environment. Career is important for income, esteem and wellbeing. Unfortunately, the pursuit of work including efforts at overcoming the barriers presented earlier can cause loss of focus on personal and family lives. The resulting imbalance can threaten the ability to achieve career goals. Many immigrants are caught up in this dilemma. People commonly experience workplace issues including discrimination, bullying, harassment, unfair dismissal, and unsafe work conditions. These situations have often derailed the careers of newcomers who are mostly unaware of their workplace rights and are not skilled enough to engage with employers in arguing their cases. Global factors also threaten jobs and careers. Some recent ones are the global financial crisis 2009, the oil price slump 2014-2016, and COVID-19 Pandemic 2020. People of all backgrounds are impacted. Immigrants are particularly vulnerable due to the factors already highlighted in this book.	As immigrants: Firstly, acknowledge that these situations will happen. There is little you can do to stop their occurrence or hasten them to finish. Maintain physical, mental and spiritual wellness during such situations. Build a strong friendship and network base for survival and progress. Build robustness and contingencies into your skillset. Activate different skills and qualifications as the dispensation demands. Educate yourself and be aware of your rights. Exercise them boldly!

4.2.4 How to Adapt in sustaining your Career

It is necessary to continue to make adjustments in your career to suit your goals in the context of your SWOTs. Indeed situations will continue to change especially with regards to the external factors which will keep driving changes to opportunities and threats in workplaces, the country, and the world. These adaptations will mostly continue all through to retirement.

Let us revisit our case study once again – the now 38-year-old immigrant from Africa with years of work experience in construction projects. He relocated to Australia on a skilled migration visa to permanently live in the new country. He has now spent about one year still seeking employment in the construction industry while doing "survival jobs" by the side to earn income for everyday living including taking care of his family.

This was his career goal with relocation in mind:

> *To secure a role as a project manager within the first six months of relocation which will help generate enough income to care for myself, my family, and still have enough at retirement for high-end lifestyle post-retirement.*

The goal needs revisiting. It is past 6 months, no project manager role, and he may not be generating enough income as planned from the "survival job." Without getting into the details of his strategic analysis the

> *"You just can't beat the person who never gives up."*
> — *Babe Ruth*

exercise will depend on a lot of factors. However, he should refresh his SWOT analysis and reset his goals including the timeline. Most importantly, he should not give up on his goals and aspirations.

Even where things are going according to plan, he will still need to revisit his career goals and plans. Continuous adjustments and improvements are required especially in those 4 key areas of communication, qualifications, work experiences and networking. He should continue to build on his strengths and taking actions to bridge gaps, seize opportunities and mitigate risks.

Communication will naturally get better over time. However, he would play a key role in his continuous improvement including getting some help if necessary. For example, he could join a local Toastmasters International or similar social clubs that can provide a 'safe' and non-judgmental environment for acquiring and improving his communication skills. He can also work with mentors that will help him learn the act of understanding the communication styles in workplaces and adjusting accordingly. Ultimately, it is about making his presence positively felt at work. It is *showing up* when and where necessary. This does not mean showing off in that other negative sense. Rather, it is the act of effective communication during workplace conversations, team interactions, managing upwards and downwards, etc.

The situation with qualifications is usually very tricky for immigrants even when they have been in the new countries for a while. It is difficult to just dump their hard-earned certificates. But it comes to that reality sometimes. The man in our case study has bachelor and master degrees in Engineering though he has spent most of his working experiences in projects. He could explore a professional certification in project management or training in software that is highly used in the industry. However, it is advisable to ensure that such certifications or software are affordable, that they are in high demand in the industry, and thus, will enhance his chances of being recruited. It is also strategic to ensure that he has a place (even a volunteer role) to use this certification or software while waiting for employment. Otherwise, he could face the risk of forgetting how to use them by the time he secures a job.

Let us consider a very important topic that requires adaptation for many immigrants: our attitude toward trades qualifications as an optional pathway to a sustainable career and income. Many immigrants have grown up in sociocultural contexts where trades like carpentry, plumbing, painting, tiling, bricklaying, etc. are considered as 'low jobs.' One will be taking a big risk to suggest to a parent that their children could consider such options! So these countries have experienced situations where significant numbers of highly qualified university graduates chase very few job opportunities. Compare this to the situations in many countries in the Western world like Australia where the secondary education system officially prepares graduating students with the option of going straight to trades apprenticeship programs of their choices. Often, they commence working and earning an income while on training. They would have acquired significant work experience and saved income very early in their careers. This gives them an edge over their counterparts that went straight to the university. Of course, there are exceptions.

Immigrants can adopt this optional pathway of Trades. Many industries and organisations with technical operations place more premium on employees and potential employees that have trades related qualifications and training compared to university graduates. This may not apply to the immigrant in our case study. However, it is still worth exploring the option. Overall, getting involved in trades will require a significant shift in mindsets for many immigrants. But the reality in many western countries is that these tradies are bosses of many very qualified people especially for roles that require more hands-on experience. Thus, organisations with such operations would place more value on trade qualifications plus relevant work experiences compared to a university qualified person with up to 3 master degrees with little or no practical work experiences like the cases we have from many countries in less developed economies. Immigrants should explore the trades culture in a way that is relevant to individual circumstances rather than deny the realities. This is an option for career adaptation and sustainable employment.

The issue of work experience is an ongoing and common challenge for immigrants in most parts of the Western world. Organisations place more weight on work experiences (especially those acquire locally) than academic qualifications. This is an ongoing reality even after securing your first job and you want to move to another job for one reason or the other. Thus, as with our case study, many newcomers would end up doing "survival jobs" while waiting to secure their first employment in the role and work level for which they have studied and acquired additional training.

Unfortunately, there is a growing trend of getting stuck in these "survival jobs" for understandable reasons but to the detriment of career goals and dreams. For some people in this situation, they could just be okay to continue. However, for many others like the subject in our case study, this would remain a source and sense of loss and he would need this resolved sooner than later. The other long term challenge is keeping the right balance between the pursuit of dreams and reality of current need for cash flow including fixed commitments like taking care of a young and growing family, paying rent, utility bills, etc. which again fits the situation with our case study. Finally, the dilemma of this situation is further compounded by the limitation of time to maintain the current job in hand as well as taking actions to secure the job of their professional callings. How can they find time for keeping their qualification current, undertaking relevant work experiences including volunteering, and networking to retain relevance in the industry of interest? It is challenging. Again, let's borrow Babe Ruth's texts: "you just can't beat the person who never gives up." Giving up should not be an option.

The situation calls for decisiveness, discipline, courage, and of course, adaptability. There is also a need for accountability including working with a mentor or mentorship program. The other option is to seek for work experience in regional areas where demand for employees are sometimes higher than supply. Moreover, the survival jobs are also available in these regions so you can sort out the cash flow challenges while pursuing your efforts in securing a role that aligns with your dream career. This is particularly suitable for young families as one of the barriers to this option is finding suitable schools for children of older ages. Thankfully, the family can work their way back to the bigger city with time as soon as that initial barrier of securing the preferred job is crossed and the skilled immigrant will now have marketable work experiences to consolidate their career goals and progression. Indeed, things do change for the better with the right attitude, efforts and adaptability.

Finally, the aspect of professional networking also goes beyond the initial adoption of the prevailing culture by immigrants on arrival into the new country. The act of networking should be refined and developed over time as this will be required not only to secure the first job, it is also necessary for sustaining your job as well as for promotion in the same organization or via taking up a new job in another organization. One needs to tap into one's wealth of networks much more for the next career move than what was required for the first job. Consider this as a pyramidal structure where the number of slots in a typical organizational chart gets less as you go higher. Consequently, competition may be higher. Thus, more references are required from the upper echelon to be selected for such roles.

Just like the need for words from your network is required for promotion, it is also applicable to avoid being caught up on the wrong side of restructures, downsizings, etc. It may look like a mystery to some outsiders regarding how workers are selected for redundancies and terminations, especially during crises like the economic downturns in 2009 (global financial crisis), 2014-2016 (oil price slump) and 2020 (COVID-19 pandemic). Invariably, people make the selection. There may be some standard yardsticks like job types (for example if your role is directly tied to the department being closed down), historical performances, formally issued warning letters (which could be due to various reasons), etc. Ultimately, people do the selection of who is to be served the letter of redundancy, termination, etc.

Thus, networking does not stop until you stop working i.e. retirement. Get to know the values of your organisation, know the key personnel (sometimes they may not be the big bosses), understand how things work including the 'politics,' and align yourself accordingly. Get yourself into strategic coffee catch-ups with colleagues, go to the pub if you can and as much as you can afford (we are all different). Most importantly, do your job so well that it will take a lot for any boss, department, or even the organization to do without you. It seems like a cliché, but it works reasonably well.

4.2.5 Achieve your professional & career goals!

What does the definition of success look like in terms of your career? This is one aspect that is challenging or could even be offensive if one prescribes a one size fits all definition of success. It is very contextual.

However, let us present some principles in line with our ongoing flow of thoughts and using the same case study goal:

> *To secure a role as a project manager within the first six months of relocation which will help generate enough income to care for myself, my family, and still have enough at retirement for a high-end lifestyle post-retirement.*

Next, we present 3 relatable scenarios of achievements in the contexts of this goal and aspects of adoption and adaptation presented in earlier sections.

Firstly, the immigrant secured their dream project management job within a year and kept making giant leaps on the job including involvement in exciting projects. He also received regular promotions, bonuses, pay increases, and a salary and superannuation (or employment funded pension) that will fund a high standard of living for him and his family post-retirement. To cap it up, he has enjoyed relatively stable health, a rich relationship with family and friends, and a positive impact in the community.

The second scenario consists of one that got to the set goal at the end, but the road has been very turbulent zigzag, requiring many adaptations and frustrations along the way. This is the one that would have had to do many survival jobs, was out of jobs many times, possibly experienced challenges to health and family with little or no positive impact in the community. The scars would be there as evidences of the toil, some obvious and others, not so visible. But the worker got there eventually. Moreover, he never really secured a project manager role but ended up as an Assistant at his peak. There were not so many bonuses, promotions, and big earnings and pension like the first scenario. Arguably, this is the most common scenario of immigrant stories.

The final and least likely scenario is a situation where the immigrant gave up and went back to his country of origin. Many times, this happens when they had kept that option open and may have had their jobs reserved for them. They would have also balanced the opportunity cost of having to go through the required processes of adoption and adaption as presented earlier in previous sections. This is being presented here as a form of achievement as well in that the person has made a decision based on considerations best known to him. Hopefully, there are some lessons learned in the process.

Many factors ultimately go into consideration for success in terms of the big move of emigrating to another country and starting life all over again. Often, intending immigrants do not take a long term view regarding the final decision to take the giant leap. Ageing is one aspect that may not have been on the minds of many people in this context.

4.3 Ageing

The conversation on the topic of ageing is still a relatively new terrain amongst immigrants especially those from new and emerging communities. However, it is one aspect of life that everyone would have to unavoidably embrace. It is a key consideration regarding how immigrants can adopt their new countries of residence, adapt where necessary, and achieve their set goals. But really, how often do people set goals for this phase of their lives? Successful and sustainable ageing are key indicators of success for anyone for that matter. However, immigrants are the primary focus of this book.

The Western world provides better opportunities for people (including immigrants) to live longer and healthier. Seniors have age-appropriate access to quality health care, social infrastructure, and stress-free access to pension and associated benefits including discounts to services and entertainment like restaurants, cinemas, gymnasiums, sports, zoos, etc. Such healthy ageing and care contribute to wellbeing and the capacity to remain mobile, building and maintaining relationships, and contributing to society.

However, it is the general expectation of new first-generation immigrants that their children will reciprocate in caring for them during their much older years of living. It is like a psychological contract between parents and their children signed and executed in the name of "our culture." After all, most of these first-generation immigrants from collectivist backgrounds did grow up in sociocultural context where this was the norm. Some are even hopeful that their children will host and care for them daily at old age rather than the alternative of being relocated to an aged care facility.

The situation in the Western world is mostly different and this triggers the need for immigrants to adopt the established system they have met in their new countries. Sometimes, they are left with very limited and affordable alternative options despite preferences. Again, let us use Australia as a case study (www.myagedcare.gov.au/). The prevalent practice is that most elderly folks will spend most of their final years on earth in their own homes (with scheduled home care services) or aged care facilities.

Aged care facilities (include nursing homes) provide residential accommodation with health care for the elderly and frail who can no longer continue living in their own homes. Residents get assistance with day-to-day tasks like meals, cleaning and laundry. They also receive personal care like showering and going to the toilet, dressing and grooming. Other services provided include 24-hour nursing care from qualified nursing staff, including managing their medications, continence care, treatment and care of wounds, and care of catheters where applicable. Many aged care homes also provide more specialised health and medical care including dementia care, palliative care, and rehabilitation.

Most ageing immigrants are indeed adopting the highly subsidized and high-quality care obtainable in the Western world. This is the case with Australia where the system is much better than the alternatives of what is available if immigrants choose the option of going back to their countries of birth to live out the latter part of their existences. However, these relative advantages have not stopped the clamour for more culturally appropriate care options which are especially sought after by people of multicultural and migrant backgrounds.

The lack of culturally appropriate meals on the menu is one aspect that has made some people or migrant and multicultural backgrounds to dread going into aged care facilities in the west. Rarely are people from such backgrounds able to fully adjust to living on food from the west. Personal care by strangers that involves so many intimate aspects like showering and going to the toilet is another challenging aspect for immigrants to adopt. The situation is further compounded for some ageing immigrants when they envisage that carers would be of the opposite sex sometimes. This is not acceptable in some cultures. It becomes apparent that these cultural norms are deeply ingrained when they come to this stage of life. It is so confronting for some people that it indeed triggers real consideration of the alternative of returning to their homelands.

The dilemma is captured in this quote from the report of the International Federation on Aging:[11]

> *The experience of caregiving and expectations regarding the appropriateness of service access are often similar for caregivers across cultures. Equally, access to and provision of formal health care and social services that are culturally appropriate can be difficult for caregivers from different countries of origin because of challenges on both sides of the exchange. Immigrants may be unfamiliar with the health and social care system and face barriers due to racism, lack of fluency in English and unavailability of culturally appropriate professional care options while cultural stereotypes may influence the attitudes and behaviours of health and social care professionals. (Dunbrack, 2005).*

Thankfully, some culturally appropriate practices are now being incorporated into aged care training curriculums and are offered as optional features in

---

[11] https://ifa.ngo/publication/social-inclusion-and-integration/enquiring-about-family-caregiving-and-their-cultural-differences/, p.5

many care facilities. Some ethnic communities have also taken the initiatives of setting up their age care facilities where culturally appropriate services that are relevant to members of their communities are offered as part of their core services. Members of the Greek and Italian communities started arriving in Australia back in the 1950s. There are now numerous aged care facilities in the country that are affiliated with these communities. One could arguably conclude that they have found their state of equilibrium with regards to ageing and aged care.

Predictably, other new and emerging immigrant communities will also go in the direction of the likes of the Greek and Italian communities as they are faced with the increasing reality of their ageing population and the need for culturally appropriate care. In the meantime, immigrants have adopted the reality of ageing and dying in the Western world. Many governments (Australia's definitely) are responsive to the need to care for the older generation. There is a general alignment in all stakeholders in the community – government and policymakers, service providers, the younger generation, and the seniors themselves – that it makes logical and moral sense to care for people that have cared for us over the past years by working and paying tax that sustained the economy to date. Efforts are truly made to ensure that people age with dignity.

This section on Ageing has not been as voluminous and structured as those on family and career for 3 reasons. Firstly, the author considers himself to be less experienced in the matter of ageing which generally commences after the retirement age of between 63 and 68 in most countries. He is not in that age bracket yet. Thus, he has only provided basic information in this book based on his observations, learning from service providers, interactions with diverse members of the community including immigrants themselves, and a bit of research. Secondly, the narratives about ageing in new and emerging immigrant communities are still at infancy stages partly because the older folks in these communities are significantly lower in number compared to other mainstream communities. Finally, the requirements and actions to adopt, adapt and achieve are mostly seamless when it comes to ageing. The system is highly regulated so that immigrants are left with little or no option but to flow with what is obtainable in their new countries of residence.

The subject of ageing is a hot topic for everyone. It is particularly relevant because it is the phase of our lives when we increasingly require support from others rather than doing things ourselves. Independence will make way for dependence, and this could be very confronting for some people including those of immigrant backgrounds. The ageing phase of life is like another "migration" to an aged care facility. Many may be facing the same challenges of relocation, change and integration but in a different context of ageing. This time around, one is more dependent and less mobile, more of the decisions may be made for us, and the capacity for adaptation may be less. We must be ready to face this phase of life with an openness of minds and willingness to accept support. Again, immigrants should tap into their strength of resilience, and hope that things will turn out well. They did it before with taking the giant leap of emigrating from the relatively known to the unknown and survived. They can do it again, this time, with ageing.

5 Concluding Remarks

All stakeholders in immigration have their reasons for such a significant undertaking. The wealth, progress and evolving identity of a country like Australia has been built on immigration. This is similar to many countries that have grown to be multicultural. Immigrants have largely influenced the economic, social and cultural aspects of the countries including contribution to economic development, wealth creation, cultural enrichment, sports, etc. Immigration is that important!

However, the immigrants themselves have been the focus of this book - how they can be more successful and sustainable in the processes and dynamics of relocation, change and integration.

It is definitely not business as usual following on from the decision to make the big move. Immigrants will necessarily undergo various forms of adopting the new country, adapting along the way, and achieving the goals they have set for themselves. The processes and experiences using this Triple A guide will be different for each immigrant but the principles and guidelines will apply to most of the readers and users, most of the time.

The immigrant will not undertake this major change of relocating and living permanently in a new country without foreseeable benefits. Often, they will voluntarily embark on the move in pursuit of career, family reunion, business, better standard of living, etc. Even when it is not voluntary like the case of humanitarian migration including refugees and asylum seekers, there are always beneficial propositions as part of the decision making processes. Moreover, many immigrants that came into the Western world on humanitarian status ended up staying permanently. There are benefits of immigration for immigrants!

The dilemma with immigrant families especially those of first-generation immigrants are very topical, raw, and prevalent. It is undeniable that most parts of the Western world provide the benefits of a relatively more stable environment for raising families. However, the associated challenges as presented in this book have become quite overwhelming for many immigrant families that sometimes it seems like a lost battle. Some of the issues are so culturally specific that relevant government officials may not have ready solutions even with funding or traditional interventions. Remarkably, the impacts will only begin to show after a long time especially for members of new and emerging immigrant communities. The Triple A guide in this book provides some principles and tools for sustainable adoption and adaptation in achieving family goals even with these challenges. The situation requires leadership from the immigrant families and communities themselves especially with providing at least the second-generation immigrants with the best foundation, tools and hope for the future. We all are better off when we have wholesome people (products of wholesome families) driving the engines of our sustainable future.

Professional pursuits and career life is another aspect with mixed narratives of benefits and challenges for immigrants just like the family context. When can skilled immigrants just come in and get on to doing what they plan to do and what they indeed do best? When can we stop the unconscious biases that may have discriminated against immigrant candidates based on their names, accents, place of study, qualifications, lack of local work experiences, and lack of 'known' references? Hopefully, the Triple A guide in this book will further enhance successful adoption and adaptation regarding prevalent practices in the corporate world in the west and ensuring more successes in careers and business entrepreneurship for immigrants.

Ageing is a human thing. However, some of the peculiarity associated with aged care for immigrants that have been highlighted in this book should provide further thoughts and considerations for adopting, adapting and integrating into the care system in the west. Some of the aspects of ageing are specific to individuals. Indeed, everyone deserves to age with dignity. Equity demands that people be given the care they prefer as long as the requirements are within the boundaries of legality and affordability.

It is not an indication of weakness to explore how to successfully adopt and adapt in your new country of residence as an intending, new or relatively more settled immigrant. Rather, having the knowledge and capacity gives you a competitive edge over those that do not seek wisdom. The content of this book has hopefully contributed to that knowledge and capacity for immigrants and other relevant stakeholders.

Other Books by
Ephraim Osaghae MBL, PMP, MBA

A

HANDBOOK
FOR
MIGRANTS

The Good, The Challenges,
and The Lessons

Ephraim Osaghae

A Reflective Guide for Meaningful and Whole-Life Experience

VOICES FROM
Home

A NARRATION OF PARENTS OF FIRST-GENERATION MIGRANTS

WISDOM FROM OUR DIASPORIC ROOTS

EPHRAIM OSAGHAE MBL

A HANDBOOK
for
MIGRANT YOUTH

PEER TO PEER WISDOM FROM THOSE WHO'VE BEEN THERE, DONE THAT

LiME Youth

Compiled by Ephraim Osaghae